SAY Bismi

Published by Ali Gator Productions.

First Published 2017

National Library of Australia Cataloguing-in-Publication (CIP) data:
Ahmad Zakky, Say Bismillah
ISBN 978-1-921772-41-2
For primary school age, Juvenile fiction, Dewey Number: 823.92

T: +61 (3) 9386 2771 **F:** +61 (3) 9478 8854
P.O. Box 2536, Regent West, Melbourne Victoria, 3072 Australia
E: info@ali-gator.com **W:** www.ali-gator.com

Yasmeen was so proud of herself. She had bought everyone donuts to share as a treat.

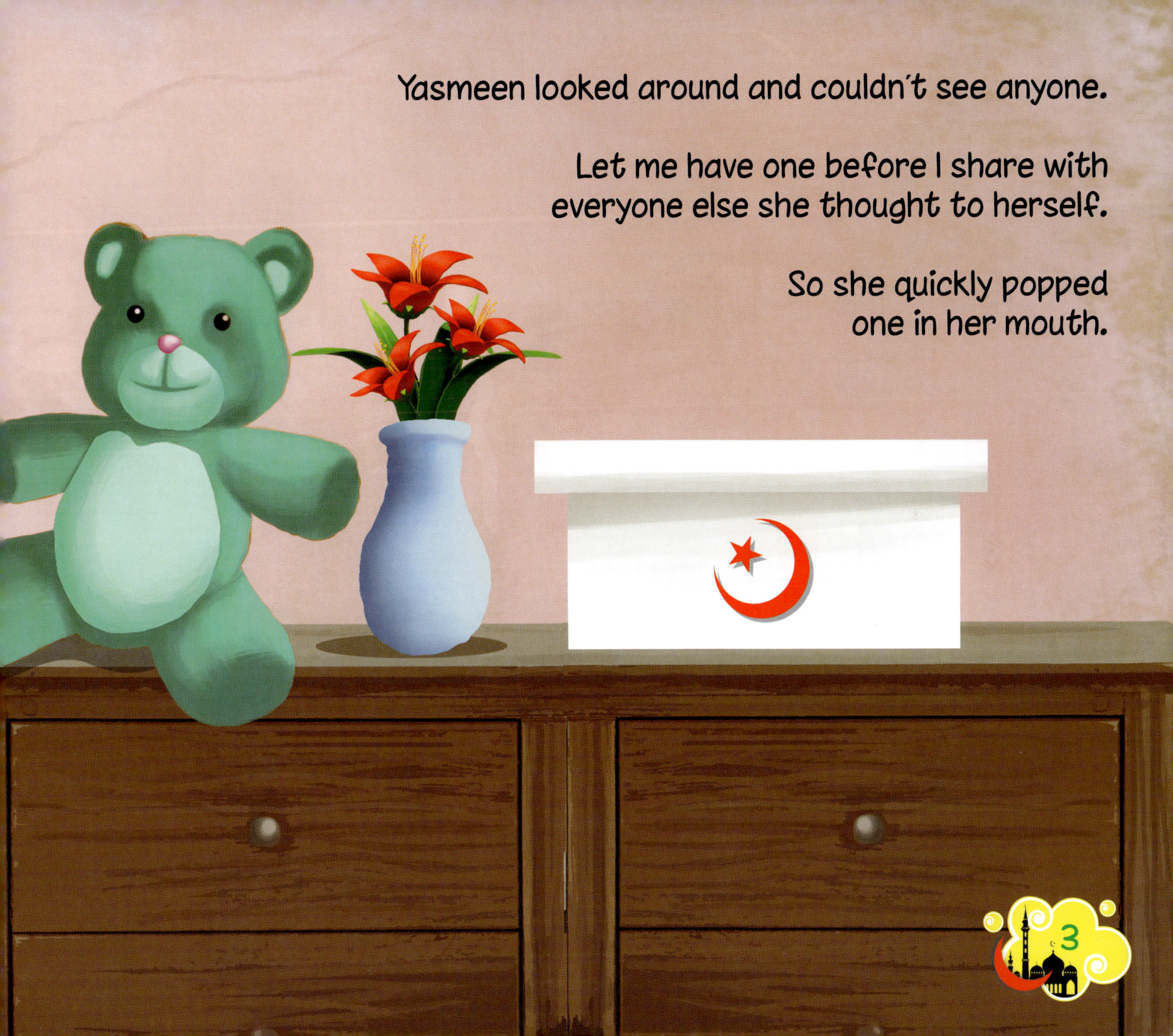

Yasmeen looked around and couldn't see anyone.

Let me have one before I share with everyone else she thought to herself.

So she quickly popped one in her mouth.

Suddenly, Yasmeen started to choke,
"Cough... Cough."

"Astaghfirullah, I forgot to say **Bismillah**,"
she mumbled to herself.

ASTAGHFIRULLAH - I SEEK FORGIVENESS FROM ALLAH
BISMILLAH - IN THE NAME OF ALLAH

"**Bismillah, Bismillah,**"
she quickly said aloud.

Once Yasmeen had recovered, she took the donuts to share with the rest of the family.

"Abdul, would you like a donut?" offered Yasmeen.

"Remember before you eat..." Yasmeen tried to tell Abdul.

But before she could get the words out Abdul took a big bite, without saying **Bismillah**.

Abdul also started to choke as he ate the donut too quickly.

"Abdul, before you eat, you must remember to first say **Bismillah**," reminded Yasmeen to her little brother.

"I was trying to tell you that, but you didn't listen," she added.

"Sit down and have some water, that will help your coughing go away," offered Yasmeen.

"What's happening in here?" asked their mother as she walked in the room.

Yasmeen was quick to explain.

"Abdul was choking on his donut, he didn't say **Bismillah**.

I tried to tell him, but he wouldn't listen," trying not to get herself in trouble.

Abdul was all confused.

He knew he was in trouble, but he didn't know why.

Was it for eating the donut too quickly?
for not listening to his sister?
or not saying **Bismillah**?

"Abdul, I've told you many times, you have to eat your food slowly and always say **Bismillah** before you eat anything," explained his mother.

"If you can Abdul, it's better to say, "**Bismillaahir Rahmaanir Raheem**," added his mother.

BISMILLAHIR RAHMANIR RAHEEM
IN THE NAME OF ALLAH, MOST GRACIOUS, MOST MERCIFUL

"I know what that means," said Yasmeen.

"**Bismillaahir Rahmaanir Raheem** means In the name of Allah, Most Gracious, Most Merciful," explained Yasmeen proudly.

Abdul, still a little confused asked his mother.

"So if I want to eat something, I must first say **Bismillah**?"

"Not only before eating, but before we start anything.

That's the lesson from our Prophet Muhammad (PBUH). He taught us that before we do anything we should say **Bismillah**."

PBUH - PEACE BE UPON HIM

"So if I want to tease Yasmeen, should I say **Bismillah**?" asked Abdul.

"No, **Bismillah** is only for good things. Teasing other people is a bad thing. You know you shouldn't tease your sister," explained their mother calmly.

Abdul nodded his head to show that he understood.

"But why should we say **Bismillah** before we start to do something?" asked Yasmeen.

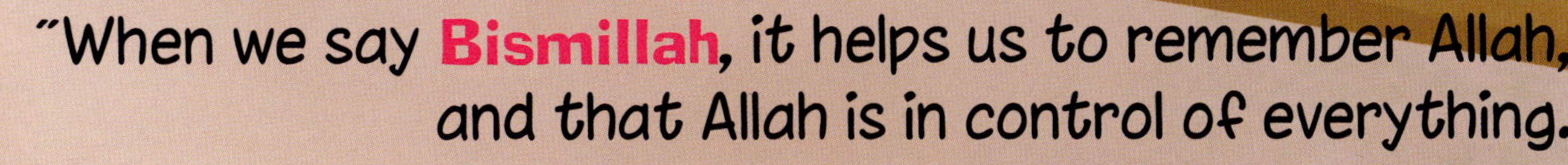

"When we say **Bismillah**, it helps us to remember Allah, and that Allah is in control of everything.

By saying **Bismillah**, it will Insha Allah help us be protected from bad things, such as choking on our food," explained their mother.

"Oh, I see. From now on, if I want to do something, I will first say **Bismillah**," said Yasmeen happily.

"Me too," said an excited Abdul, who didn't want to miss out.

The door bell rang "Assalamu Alaikum," they heard their father's voice behind the door.

"Wa Alaikum Salam," they all answered.

It was Yasmeen and Abdul's father, they were so happy to see him.

ASSALAMU ALAIKUM - PEACE BE UPON YOU
WA ALAIKUM SALAM - AND PEACE BE UPON YOU

Their father then surprised them with cold drinks he was hiding in his bag.

Both Yasmeen and Abdul were so excited.

"I'm going to say **Bismillah** before I drink," said Abdul, trying to outdo his sister.

"Me too," added Yasmeen.